21 Truths

AF624524

Angelina Vaca

BookLeaf Publishing

Presentation by *BookLeaf Publishing*

Web: www.bookleafpub.com

E-mail: info@bookleafpub.com

ISBN: 9789357211710

First edition 2023

DEDICATION

This book is for little Angelina. I love you. For the ones who love love. I love you. For the readers trying to find their story and inspiration on the pages. I love you. And definitely all my cats. Miss you Patches.

ACKNOWLEDGEMENT

I would like to thank everyone I have ever met. All the teachers in all my schools, friends I've made, enemies I hated, and people I wish I knew better. You have all taught me something important and if I don't understand the lesson yet…I will. Thank you to BookLeaf Publishing for this opportunity and challenge as an author.

PREFACE

Growing up I didn't talk a lot because I thought I never knew the right words. So I listened instead. So from years of listening, this is what was heard.

All cheesy goodness is made from Angelina Vaca.

Friday

You're my Friday
When the weather goes my way
My plans for you are strong

So I sit and wait
Counting down the days
Oh Friday you can't do wrong

Achievements

I grew up thinking I was special and precious
And all my achievements were pieces of the
superior me that I would some day become
I wanted someone to pat my back
And someone to ruffle my hair
Take a look at my plain interests
Look and remind me they're special
But I found it had to make me shy
Blush and smile at the ground
Almost like poor little me
Like I didn't know my potential

Because some people only surround you
Give you scraps of love and praise
Keeping your hate for yourself thrive
Because people love the underdogs
They get the most love
Play innocent and humble
Before they feel you're better than them

Because once they get that feeling
Things can go sideways
They'll give you compliments that feel dull
Ignore you and wave you away
Or burst into a pity party

Then demand you to give them what they are supposed to give you

All your dreams and achievements are armour
They'll get nicks and scratches
But they'll always protect the most important thing

Liar

I let you taste my lie with dew
Thought it was better for me and you
I just wanted what I wanted
"Never meant to hurt you"
If I said that I'll be lying
I was hurt don't call me conniving

My heart was heavy
My lungs were jelly
Trying to keep me up
"Sorry" wouldn't be enough
Because it had no weight
Wish things weren't filled with hate

Feelings are futile I know
They change quickly to the unknown
The guilt, the dark, the sad
I just wanted an end to the bad
The part that feels like death
God grant me your hand, save me a breath

Dolls

I sit and play with my dolls
While chatter starts down the hall
The shuffling of shoes
The creak of the door
The panic sizzles more and more

I blink and shake it off
She sits and plays but is cross
I know I'm not fun
But what can be done
When adults want to play
They send me away

How should I entertain?

School

Scream of laughter and play
Chairs rumbling and squealing on the floor
Hallways filled with strangers
Oh we're friends
Oh we aren't anymore
"Let's move onto something else"

What am I missing?

The day drags on
Doing what I should
But there's something missing
My eyes are drawn to a pair
They're full and spill with cheer
I wanna know what they're saying
But there's something that I'm missing
So I go back to what I'm doing

The next day drags on
Doing what I usually do
But there's something different
In those pair of eyes that sometimes meet
They're full and spilling of courage
I wanna know what they wanna say
But maybe I'm missing something
So I go back to what I'm doing

Another day happens to drag by
Doing what I have to do
But there's something lingering
A pair of blur well up in my eyes
My eyes' redness fades away and I wonder
But why do I have to be missing something
I swallow it down
So I can go back to what I'm doing

You're an adult now

Praise the quick wit
Give them a raise
Tell them that's it gonna okay
Waste your youthful days
Spend time with the adults
But it's still gonna be your fault
It'll start off slow, with some days your more sour
Then you can't stop crying for more than an hour
But one day it'll just click
Then you'll feel the weight brick by brick

All the things you don't know that you missed
They'll come back demanding a kiss
And when you finally throw a fit
They'll pretend they don't see it
Because they gave you a load
That you couldn't possibly hold
Now fitting in that mold hurts and gives you sores
But now it's too late, you have to finish your chores

Functional love

All the face masks and pedicures
They don't erase this stress
That my youth is depleting
And I look like a mess
I can't rewind the time again
I'm trying to stay cool and neat
But when will we finally meet

Functional love
When will I meet you
Can I get to choose
What kind of sign you show
When I'm finally your muse
And I'll always wait time and time again
Oh functional love
I imagine you in my head

The kind of love that dances in the kitchen and
in flurries of snow
The kind of love that makes me cry
Because I'll just know
That I've always been such a lucky girl
It was just time in the way
Before I can look in your eyes and promise
I'll love you like this everyday

Infinite

Kissing someone like you could be nice
A sensation that will trickle down the spine
All I can think of is finding an excuse
A way of making you feel more mine
But the anxiety steeps in
That you might not be made for me
So I tuck my wants away
Keep those fantasies in my dreams

I find myself thinking of you
Why do our eyes meet the way they do
Maybe if I knew more
I'll suddenly get bored
And move on to something with more means
Like those fantasies in my dreams

I'll find someone to love
Give them all of my heart
Who knows the time from here and then
Might not be so far apart

That's why I want it to be you
Why I want it to be true
That my forever is around the corner
And not an hour further of torture

And as much as the parts of me
Thinks that's they're ready now
They sometimes don't feel so sure
When someone with it all comes around
Oh my timing cannot be definite
But God I want a love so infinite

Addicted

I'm addicted to people like you
With stars and hope in your eyes
Hiding your glitter cause you're shy
The miles I'd run to be your escape
Let me shake your fear away

Without knowing I'd anticipated you
Wished you'd walk in the door
Thinking about last time I've seen you
Oh I can't help but adore

Everything you do melts me
At the same time keeps me on my toes
I just pray you don't hate me
I hope that's not how this goes

With us never knowing
That my pining will fade
That I'll learn to live without your glowing
But maybe that's my fate that was made

What can I do?

I can’t say I meant for you
Even though I wish that was the case
I can’t fill that space
Between your heart and the world
No matter how much it swirls
But I’ll show you that there isn’t anything
If you aren’t my everything
I would do it for you
Every chance it’s for you

Bliss

Kiss me harder
My breath is sharper
Bite my lips
Feel my skin in your finger tips

Your fingers are combing my hair
If they leave me I'll be in despair
Grind my hips
Find my heart as it skips
This must be it
My heavenly bliss

Heartbreak

Seeing you less helps until I see you again
Suddenly feel I left hell
Oh you smiled at her again
Your eyes crinkle so well

It's always the "little did you knows"
"I've thought of you for hours"
"How could they let me go"
I've built shrines and towers
For the you in my head
But I'm almost over it
Felt the shame that made me crawl in my bed
Almost over it

There's some days I wish I were
Your dream girl but then it hurts
You still could've chosen her
Would've felt like a deeper burn
Wish I could hate her with a reason to
Wish she wasn't wonderfully fashioned too

Wish and pray you'll someday leave her
Or maybe that's a new low
Maybe heartbreak will bring allure
Give me a certain glow

"Break my heart and I'll break yours"
All the boys wanna know

Her

A radiance
A beam
Her life flows out of her like a stream
Oh god when she smiles I can finally dream

Not about earthquakes or breaking hearts
A comforting truth that can't be torn apart
A sweet summer breeze priming for a celestial clear sky
For drive through take out and simple highway rides

She claims herself and the air that surrounds
With love she forgives the what ifs
Even the "but whys" and the excuses they find
They want to tamper and putter in her mind
But they cannot get what they most desire
Not during her lucky hours

At least you were consistent

You were consistent to disappointment
If only you booked a stupid fucking appointment
To stitch my heart back again
Now it's my problem once again

You were consistent to disappointment
To apply the stinging ointment
To wipe it off and apply it again
Now it's my problem once again

You were consistent to disappointment
So quick to appear for my anointment
Just to show up late because I didn't remind you
again
Now it's my problem once again

You were consistent to disappointment
So I did something disliked and you pointed
Leaving me to teach you once again
Not once was it my problem to tend

Now it doesn't

I worked so hard for it not to hurt
I shamed and guilted and prayed
I fought so hard for them to go away
For them not to stay

Now this emptiness confuses me
I can't tell if it's really bad
But freedom fuses into me
So I take it with a grain of sand

I can't believe I am finally here
A space in my mind you cannot fray
I wish I knew how I did it
How now I don't owe you any pay

Sometimes they trickle in
They don't get too far
But they're too fickle to steer me
Too weak to mark

Maybe one day we will talk about it
Pain to pain
For now I'll grow out of it
Day by day

Power

There's power in your walking and talking
Your silence, your stillness, your flaunting
There's power in your stand, your huddle
Your bruises, your punches, your cuddles
There's power in your ever changing existence
Your heart's beating persistence
There's power in your sadness, your grief
Your silliness, your relief
Embrace the power that you naturally have
Not the value that someone has halved
Don't ignore your power or it will haunt you
People will see it and find an excuse to taunt you
There's power in you that's yours
It didn't choose you but forever's yours

If I was enough

If I was enough
If I was whole
What would I buy
What would I wear
Would I still be shy
Would I still care

If I was enough
If I was whole
What would I drive
What would I know
How would I know
Where would I go

If I was enough
If I was whole
What would I lie about
What would step on my toes
Would my highs be high
Would I still have lows

If I was enough
If I was whole
Who would I know
And who wouldn't know

Death

Death has been my friend for as long as I've
been born
Living in my dying cells while I'm still
breathing
Visiting the bird twitching in my hand
Leaving the cat that the car should've skimmed
over
And a sting of fear like meeting a potential lover

Because the heart, it feels still
But stillness isn't only meant for death
That's something I've learned
It's meant for anger, fear or shock
And suddenness isn't only meant for death
It's something people yearned for
It's meant for jokes, realizations or miracles

Moreover, don't search for death
Because it'll always introduces first
And if your need is still there
There's a crumb of death around you

Cured

It's been a while but more smiling has happened
Maybe brighter than I've imagined
You've been busy and I've been too
Slightly happy I haven't seen you
My hearts not skipping
I think I'm almost cured
If I see you I surely won't be turned
So I wait again to see you
Almost sure it's true
And look at that, I survived without you

I see specks of you throughout the days
And I make it without obsessing
Last time I'm not so lucky and so I'm in a haze
Hope I don't miss my moment of confessing
Looking at your eyes and all I see is the truthful truth
That I don't know how to get over you even if was for you

Now I sit here and ponder what was going through your gorgeous eyes
While you stared at mine that one time
Oh she's so native
She's gonna try an' fix a broken piece

But that's not what you need
What do I need

Okay fine I played the game
Where seeing you fanned a flame
And I was stuck and now I'm asking
What the fuck

I pined and I weeped
Lost time meant for sleep
For someone who couldn't pick
I'm tired of trying
To figure out how you tick

You can throw me to the fire
Call me a dirty liar
I can't keep trying or I'm going to lose
It's not me when it's you
Who can barely fucking choose

Something better

No one would tell me that I just needed love
And when I reached the need will grow above
And soon I would be unsatisfied and selfish
No matter how I was cherished
When I met them I thought I just I had to wait
It didn't matter my state
For them to change was them being kind
And if I was second I didn't mind
And if they stayed with me the longest
Thought without them I will be the smallest
It was supposed to be obvious
But I was just oblivious

And it still hurt when their damage was gone
Could see the darkness in my eyes dawned
I became delusional so I can stop blaming me
And I started to see different parts of me

Spent a long time avoiding the need creeping up
And slipping down my nerves almost giving up
The feeling of something missing
So at the tip of my tongue it sits
Until something just clicks

Now I can't look away

The symptoms drawing together
Like a brush stroke on a page
My bursts of energy explained
The knot in my throat when I see the seconds change
I know where my control lies
What wasn't truly mine and with not much time
I'm finally alive
I've come to claim what is mine

www.ingramcontent.com/pod-product-compliance
Lightning Source LLC
Chambersburg PA
CBHW062109140826
49812CB00058B/1101
9789357211710